A FUTURE
REMEMBERED

A Future Remembered

A Journey Tapping into A Natural Order

Krystal Kelley

Contents

A s I sit down to write this prologue in quarantine April, 2020; the quantum crown virus has initiated another major energy shift. I reflect on that energy portal we opened in 2011 and the subsequent two week isolated quarantine I had in Siberia's Altai Mountains. Here, I try to connect some dots for the reader.

My journals ran over the years from 1988 until somewhen in 2008. I used to document almost daily thoughts, actions and events that happened. In 2008, I did something different. I read them. Before this, they had collected dust as I moved the bin of journals with me from house to house. I read them chronologically and they were surprisingly....boring. But, I realized something BIG. My writing was a good insight into how my mind was mapping a reality that I was presently living within. I realized that I was writing the directives that were shaping my future self.

Inspired by the power I held in my hands, heart and mind, I decided to take action on this power. I began writing more creatively and less structured. I adopted a motto, "I'll go where the day takes me". This story is a journey of where my days have miraculously taken me. My ultimate creative expression is told in loving unison with cosmic reality. I have changed some names and taken creative license with fuzzy memories. You will notice that my past, present and future tense is all over the place. This is intentional. Time occurs in more than one dimension, so you will find that throughout this manuscript, you will transcend time through my mazy mind. I hope everyone can keep up.

I encourage you to read the footnotes of this book. They contain direct wisdoms channeled through many of the light workers I have had the pleasure and divine opportunity to work directly with. My deepest gratitude goes out to all my family and friends that have supported all my seemingly crazy ideas, yet they support my energy wholeheartedly. A creative project such as this might have started with an idea that I had, but it is not possible to come to fruition without the collective support our fellow artists. I need to extend a special thank you and gratitude from my WHOLE heart to Peter Van Hetzel (Peter the Great), Chris Hildebrand, Maia Rose, Karah Pino, Luna Katynova and David Walega. Especially to our amazing trek leader who bravely forged the path from Seattle to Altai, Carol Hiltner. Carol essentially brought all of us together to carry out this amazing and powerful energy work to heal our Mother, our planet, our home: Earth.

Lastly, I want to explain the sketches interwoven into the chapters. The ink and paper sketches before each chapter are "drawn without drawing" by Peter the Great. The acrylic sketches illustrate the reverberations of other dimensions that occur throughout the story. The art was crafted by David Walega.

Existential Home

Remodeled framework of a life lived before,

A roof framing events we adore,

Memories stored in rooms,

Swept away by brooms.

We fill the space with ornament,

A pathological reflection of our lament.

The things we see

become what will be.

Part I

Discovering the Natural Order

I sit looking at the Earth from a vessel, the vessel that held the message all along. This one life has flown by, but I've had many; a long Akashic memory of natural, chaotic patterns. I was Empress Matilda, a legitimate heir to the English Throne, I am now a Mom in America, I will one day attend a Galactic Conference on another star…I am indigenous to my galaxy. I'm ignited by electricity with three eyes to see and one heart to feel…the galaxy has changed. Occupy movements cataclysmically erupted throughout the universe. Was this a direct result of our energy work we did at the navel of planet Earth?

That remote wilderness in the Siberian, Altai Mountains. Or was it purely a coincidence? No one will ever know... the future blindfolds us, entrusting us to rely on our eyes and the feeling in our heart to guide us. Intuition and intention become the tools to shape our future. This web I have been weaving is about to connect with all beings in all dimensions to become one gloriously woven fabric of the future.

Time Machine

Backwards or forwards;

Time occurs in more than one dimension.

Simple transcendence through the mazy mind;

Time is eternally ephemeral.

The Earth was slowly slipping between the sun and the moon and I was taking the garbage out. The lunar surface was a tint of orange and the damp air chilled me to goose-bumps. It started raining harder and I wondered how I could see the full moon through the layers of clouds? The moon was so bright! I heard it had been 372 years since a lunar eclipse occurred on the winter solstice, yet I had a déjà vu. One of my past lives tickling my memory.

Vibrations in some kind of dimension that I can't explain have always made taking out the garbage exciting. How is that? What a mundane task, but it was not a mundane day. This day, March 12, 2012 was the opening of Mind Unwind, a Seattle art gallery. The opening of the gallery was a ridiculous, random and radically coinciding event within this prism of a holographic universe that I was reverberating inside of. Even now, years later, I look back at the gallery and wonder, was it fantasy? A dream? Or was the gallery just a reality created by this "crystal" pen that I grasp in my hand?? I'm not sure, but either way, I like all those possibilities.

Perspective. What you see at first isn't always what is there. Right now, you see a square. Ideas ripple, sound vibrates and that square spins and spins...until all you see is a circle. Tomorrow, your square may become a circle. That circle becomes a cone and eventually you see the prism that creates our holographic universe. How do we believe what we see?

Now

All that is, is now.

The past lies in a network of memories.

Dendrites twisted amongst each other;

Like a nautical ball of rope tossed ashore in a storm.

The future lies within the network of my dreams;

Disentangling my nautical rope after the storm clears.

Intuition and action are now.

Let me finish with the garbage and I will take you to the ocean's shore. To a spot I choose as the beginning. A beginning suggests an ending, but we are just circles of light vibrating in this space. Alas, to start "somewhere": From disaster to storm to ongoing and expanding synchronistic events, the shifting circles of the mist continue to expand and may wrap around you too. So read carefully and keep notes. I am certain if you are reading this, then you too have a part in the circle of this ongoing story.

Chapter 1

Mind Unwinding

felt the Earth shake that morning; in fact I had felt it shaking almost 24 hours before the actual earthquake. Was it a premonition, a feeling, or just my imagination happening to be accurate? It makes little difference now, but I had known.

Of the millions of possibilities of places to be in one's life, I found myself at the very Western edge of the Pacific Ocean in the very small town of Westport, Washington. The swelling surf of the Pacific was separated from my building only by a large rock jetty. The jetty was home to hundreds of feral cats. The Great Japan Tohoku Earthquake of March 11, 2011 was about to occur.

I work in real estate and some years prior, I had a client who owned this property in Westport. It was called "Pelican Point" and over the years had been home to a popular pizza spot for tourists. The pizza place closed down and a collective art gallery was sharing the space. My client needed to sell it to finance other projects and on a whim; my ex-partner (the surfer) and I purchased Pelican Point. The building was in the marina of Westport, which was a long-time beach respite for Seattleites. There were pictures in one of the historical mansions in Westport that the Kennedy family would come visit the beach when on the West Coast. For the surfer, he liked the fact that Pelican Point sat right on a surf break. I was a city dweller, a real estate agent, and a serial entrepreneur of sorts. I enjoyed business, people and making money. This building was not one of those money making purchases, but I loved the history of the town and was easily persuaded to purchase it. I wanted to focus on improving the property. Fortunately or unfortunately, protecting our investment was hard when we were living in Seattle two hours away.

I am the City of Seattle. I was born and raised here and I feel the city grew up with me. My grandfather met my grandmother in Georgetown, one of the oldest neighborhoods. He was a successful, handsome real estate agent and business man. My grandmother was the 7th daughter of an immigrant family from Spain. When the Smith

Tower was the highest building west of the Mississippi, my grandfather managed the building and lived in the dome on the top of the Tower. He stood at the top of the world then. I spent a lot of time with my grandfather as a child, he was retired and I was his "favorite." Although, I'm sure he told all 14 of his grandchildren the exact same thing. As a child, I believed all of Grandpa's far-fetched stories about fishing for sharks off the pier and real estate deals that took him in his helicopter to develop the Kent Valley. He was an amazing storyteller and he made me feel like Seattle was my small town.

My best friend Yam and I would play in the forbidden woods behind her house. It started off as the neighborhood playground, but a dismembered foot was found by some other children. The police quarantined the area until the body of a young girl, another victim of the Green River serial killer, had been found. After the crime scene tape was stripped from the site, the woods were forbidden by all the parents. It was frightening to think about, but Yam and I had vivid imaginations, the courage of youth and a constant thirst for adventure.

The forbidden woods were magical. Yam and I made forts and created vast and elaborate stories and we created languages and people and kingdoms to match them. We felt we could speak to the animals and we asked them to protect us from the serial killer. In all practicality, we felt safe there and knew no one else would interrupt our playing because we were the only brave ones to reenter.

REVERBERATION 1

The Language of Subtleties

One afternoon we laid down in a bed of wild mushrooms, nature's original memory foam, the mushrooms padded us along with a pillow of sword ferns. We were watching the clouds through the fingers of the trees. There were many layers to our stories and looking back on it now, we both started to resonate with the forest vibrations, the deep, dark sounds, these clouds and connections with the creatures and trees around us.

"I see a butterfly," I say looking at the clouds taking shape in the gentle breeze.

"I see a heart" says Yam.

"Do you feel like these shapes could mean something?" I ask.

"Do you mean, like someone is speaking to us from another dimension?" asks Yam.

"Exactly what I am thinking" I concur.

At that, a creature not afraid of a serial killer slowly saunters nearby nibbling on the salmon berries. It is a baby black bear and we knew that meant the mama was close behind. Soon enough, here came mama bear. We are so nestled in the mushrooms and ferns that we don't think the bears will notice us.

We were wrong.

Mama bear walks directly towards us. Our hearts skip and we both hold our breath and grasp each other's hands.

To our surprise, she says, "Salutations chosen few."

I can't believe that I'm not running, but neither is Yam. I feel this bear is kind and gentle and she just spoke to us. Yam is quicker to respond than I am.

I'm Yamane, this is my best friend, Krystal, but she calls me Yam for short, you can too. Who are the chosen few?"

"You two. Like your grandfather, Krystal, you can see both sides of the spectrum. One day, it will all make sense." answers Mama bear.. She continues, "Listen, my children, there is your brother over there eating salmon berries, you are all children of our mother... we are all connected. An interspecies revolution will happen one day and all species, even yours, will follow the natural order. Keep this in your heart and you will continue to be protected."

Yam and I stared wide-eyed at each other...we looked back and mama bear and our new bear brother were sauntering back down towards the river. We are speechless. We get up from our mushroom bed and run home. Yam's mom, Suko, is waiting for us with rice balls and seaweed. Yam's mom was from Japan, so we only eat traditional Japanese food at Yam's house.

"Mom, we saw a bear and she spoke to us!!" yells Yam running in the open door.

"Yeah, and she was so nice. She said she protected us and her cub!" I pig-tail on Yam's excitement.

Suko looks at us puzzlingly, yet smiles, "Now, eat something. You must be starving, you were out in those woods all day AND you know you aren't supposed to be going in there!" Suko is still smiling while trying to be stern.

"We know, we know. We won't go back," we say. With crossed fingers behind our backs, Yam and I exchange a knowing glance. We know we will be back.

Our forests of youth are supposed to last, at least for a few years, but the forbidden woods were quickly developed into housing as Seattle grew into an international business center. Staying pace with Seattle, I graduated from University and my thirst for adventure quickly became global and beyond. In the end

Seattle is still who I am, and I seem to always find my way home.

END REVERBERATION

A drizzle on my cheek, the hum of wind and birds flying overhead tugs me to Seattle in 2010, where I live with my two daughters and the surfer. Again, the forest; there is an urban forest near my house, this one is not forbidden. Remarkably preserved, old growth trees reach like antennas to the universe and I found myself sitting on a fallen log. I was motionless, floating on the log in an equilibrium, I felt as if I were a satellite floating in the atmosphere. There was ineffable joy inside of me, but I was also inundated with megs of information daily; the "politricks" of society, I was over-stimulated, hypnotized by the flashing lights, the screens, "entertrainment" that lulled me into zombie-like reactions, I was craving clarity....and there I sat.

Who knows how long?

I sat,

I sat,

I sat,

I sat

and I sat.

Unwinding.. I felt myself slowing down and letting the noise of a fast life slip off of me. My mind calmed and I felt my heart beating again. Unwinding...stillness. I took my mind off of my vision, and looked without intention of seeing.

All at once, I saw sparkles in the distance, the water of Elliott Bay in front of me glistening like I had never seen before. The sun peaked out and I noticed dragonflies buzzing around my head. Two balls of light or swirls of energy appeared in front of me. Something within me knew I was looking at myself from another dimension; the pulsing energies were my own. They were torn apart yet I knew together they could be so much more powerful. A voice asked, "How do I reignite my own fire?" The smaller of the two balls of light was weakened, and the larger floated away towards the West. My mind told me what my heart knew: to the West I will go.

I had my answer!! I must move to Westport, to the edge of the Pacific Ocean, to work on our property and on myself. I'm not a runner, but propelled by my reawakened spirit I ran back to our house. Out of breath and filled with my newly rediscovered energy, I let the surfer and my children know that we were moving to the beach. It was an easy sell for the surfer....Just like that, *POOF* I up-rooted us to that tiny little beach town on the edge of the Pacific Ocean. Westport, Washington where less than a year later, the Earth would shake the world and myself full time into my expanding role in this galactic way.

Unplug

I'm taking a poll on what computers do to my soul.

I used to dream, now I only talk to a virtual screen.

Business comes in the form of a text,

It's multiple choice on what to do next.

The choices don't include love, compassion or ethos.

It's all about a money mission increasing the zeros.

It's not scientific, my poll;

But I feel the electric drain has taken a toll.

After getting settled in Westport I had time to unwind my thoughts of our life back in Seattle. The routine had been fucking with my head. The monotony was killing my spirit. I had to disconnect my thoughts from my mind to find the root of my being. Those two visions of light freed me, and it felt good. I collect treasures in moments of joy to recall when my barometer is malfunctioning. I call it my barometer of happiness, the interweaving of my being. My existence is a recall of those treasures, and I was certain I needed to break the rut of routine.

I was walking a new path, unknown rocks beneath my feet. The new, foreign and unexpected are what I needed to nestle back into my baseline. My being felt as if I had been through a long, cold winter…cocooned inside and now, I was uncloaking myself to fly again. I had released the energies that were binding me and threw them into a burning fire. The smoke had stung my eyes, tears swelled, but once flushed, I could see more clearly. Open. I now move forward with the zeal of a prisoner escaped from captivity. I have created a new path, the future's imprints unknown to me, but I feel my heart knows.

I laugh. I can't stop laughing at my silly kids. They love the beach and our new life. The surfer hasn't joined us yet. He was still in Seattle finishing up work—that's how fast we left. The house was still in escrow and details needed to be completed. For the first few weeks, everyday gave me a feeling of nirvana. Just me with my freshly freed spirit and my children at our new beach. Then, my surfer returned.

Chapter 2

Great Japan Tohoku Shakes

The very night the surfer joined us, I had a dream we were demolishing a house. That was it. A very short dream that caused me to awake from it with ice in my veins. My whole being had turned cold, like a light switch had been turned off. From rediscovering my spirit through following the mystical balls of light to suddenly having this deep and cold sensation was overwhelming. Fear swelled up in me that I had made the wrong move.

Still in bed, my mind was now being overrun with spirit messages. I could feel the earth shaking. I was told we had to get away from this shore. A tidal wave of emotions and thoughts had completely consumed me.

I calmed myself as much as I could and let the sensations pass, but the messages had been received. That spirit that I had just released from a jail of monotony was now a major player in my heart and I trusted it.

That morning, I took the girls to school and let them know I'd be back after a vacation. I left. I was done with the surfer. There was no turning back, the universe and all the vibrations were telling me I had to act.

I drove back to Seattle to start making arrangements for our immediate return. The day was March 11, 2011. I was about to enter into this very real well of still unknown depths—that fateful morning. March 11, 2011. If you remember, the earth shook to the tune of a magnitude 9.0 earthquake in Japan. Over 15,000 people died and I felt it with a magnitude inside my heart that awakened something.

That day, I was at my best friend Kate's house in Seattle, and upon awakening I didn't recognize the world. It was confusing and sad. My kids were in a potential tidal wave and seeking high ground with the surfer. I was constantly connected to them though. It was a symbiotic evolution, a lesson in telepathy and heart-felt energy. Luckily for my children and this side of the Pacific Ocean, the tidal wave feelings I had earlier never hit Westport.. The Earth, however, was badly hurt and I could feel something that sparked the overarching "mother" in me to seek a healing path--I still see the clock at 11:11 almost every day.

The dream, the waves of emotions, the flood of information coming from my spirit. It all made sense now. But what sense? Had I predicted the earthquake and tsunami? Why had my mind become so filled with dread about Westport and the ocean, and so certain of new ideas for actions? My heart was ripped open with self doubts to be separated from my children. We watched the poor Japanese shoreline being washed away by an event that I somehow felt deeply and spiritually connected to.

From that horrible and frenetic day, I no longer doubted myself and two things had become certain. The first was my freed mystical energy was very real and I had begun to be able to profoundly connect with it, the Earth and perhaps others of the same vibration.. The second certainty was I knew the courage of that girl who had played in the forbidden woods was still very much alive in me. Those energies and some new mystical faculty from beyond seemed to be guiding me somewhere for something. I had no idea how right I was or how monumental the path would be.

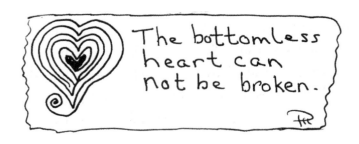

The bottomless heart can not be broken.

Chapter 3

Symbiotic Evolution

Bye Bye

So long dream,

All it makes me want to do is scream.

Hello now,

Where I'm going doesn't matter how.

Everything that happened yesteryear

Is a treasured memory I hold dear.

I live now, slow and fast—

Towards the future cause I can't change the past.

Personally, I needed to find an apartment in Seattle and get my kids back to school near me, but they had already started their school year in Westport and their dad happily could care for them until summer break. I was talking to them every day by phone and telepathically, my heart was with theirs. They were safe and I had new work that was becoming my focus . I created a motto for myself: I'll go where the day takes me.

My symbiotic evolution felt tumultuous, but I had so much clarity. As I raced through in freefall, resourcefulness and creativity built a parachute and when my parachute started to fail, I grew wings midair. Those wings became heavy, gravity collided with time and space and I followed the signs that each day appeared.

I started to take long walks and began noticing bird poops that looked like shapes to me, a heart, a bear riding a unicycle, it was an organic Rorschach test literally on my daily path. Missing my kids, I wrote a children's story about a little bird who poops art. It was an adventure book and I couldn't wait to share it with them and the world. I called the bird poops "splats". Finding splats was finding unexpected beauty in a commonplace calamity. It was hilarious and it made my days bright, even when there was darkness.

Quest ?

Pause to ponder

The echoes in your head.

Answers might reverberate.

Continue along your journey—

Until you find the question to your answer.

Can clarity come in the form of a question?

Following my daily signs of bird poops, I start to notice the most random synchronicities. For example, one day I was in a line at the grocery store. There was an old lady in front of me. After I put my items on the conveyor belt I looked up. We had the EXACT same items—the same bottle of red wine, two avocados and a dozen eggs.

Am I standing in line behind my future self? Is that conveyer belt the split between an alternate universe? My mind is wandering again into a parallel universe where I time travel to the grocery store just to see my past self. What do I say to my future self?

"Good afternoon, how is your day?" the clerk chimes in.

I look up, my future self has checked out and I'm first in line. "Unbelievable" I say.

I finished buying my wine, avocados and eggs. Darn, I really wish I had talked to her, I felt certain she was cool and had so many good stories. I vowed going forward to try not to miss opportunities that sprung up from synchronicity .

It was now April of 2011 and I traveled to Vancouver, BC visiting friends and putting Splat stickers everywhere I went.

Magical things for magical people

Chapter 4

Parallel Dimension –A Unified Field

About four months earlier to that memorable March of 2011, a man named Peter and his wife, Rui were vacationing in the Caribbean. He was working for an environmental company and his wife was a banker. The couple lived in Chicago, but had originally met through a long string of events that started with the resource starved Japanese wartime government collecting metal to scrap for the war effort. This included a buddhist temple bell from a small town in Chiba called Ohara.

After the war ended the USS Minnesota discovered the bell in a scrap yard in Yokohoma and took it as a war prize. The bell ended up in northern Minnesota, in the city hall of Duluth. In 1954 a Japanese education research team discovered the bell and thought it quite odd that this bell would be in such a place. They notified the temple back in Japan, and even though tempers were still rough, Duluth agreed to send the bell back as a symbol of peace. It was national news in both countries at the time, and naturally Duluth and the Japanese town of Ohara in Chiba became sister cities years laters. That is how Peter and Rui met. They are kind of a miracle couple and Peter, or the spirit of Peter was about to roar for the first time.

On their vacation Peter had a dream for a television show called Shifting Circles. The concept was a traveling spiritual vaudeville show. Until that December of 2010 Peter would freely admit he had lived a pretty small, but charmed life. Shifting Circles was an idea that ignited something in him and he vowed to follow it out as best he could.

Peter started to be aware of the universe opening up for him and the project was coming together. He fought his fears and just kept going forward and saying yes. For the first time in his life he was not going to be blocked. Shifting Circle's pilot show would be made. Since the pilot involved new age healers, Peter tried to prepare himself as well as he could. The learning curve was high, as he knew little of the subject and believed less than that.

About five days before leaving for Vancouver, Peter and Rui were watching a brief video on spirals of the Hopi Peoples of SW America. Rui went off to brush her teeth and Peter got up from his chair and suddenly started to feel light headed and dizzy.

He sat on the floor and the room now began to spin at a ridiculous speed. He remembers lying down and watching the TV go flying by my vision as fast as a person can move their hand.

Spin

spin

spin

spin

spinning …

Peter's stomach started to feel queasy. He cried out to Rui.

Peter closed his eyes in an effort to calm the spinning, but he needed a bucket. He completely emptied his stomach with five hellacious purges.

Rui called their doctor and he wisely guessed it probably was the video of the spirals.

As many magical experiences that were about to begin for Peter, I believe it was that spiral resetting that opened him up to what was to occur in Vancouver and beyond.

A few days later he was on his way to the Pacific Northwest and Vancouver for the production with TV producer Pat Bermel who liked the Shifting Circles concept and agreed to partner in it.

Pat had arranged to bring together seven healers to a small crystal and healing center in Britannia Beach, north of Vancouver. . The pilot plan was to film the healers giving sessions. Reiki, past lives, aroma therapy, floral healing, chakra meditations, taro, I ching, guiding saints identifications and more... all of these were completely foreign to Peter and his brother, Matt.

It was their first time to the Pacific Northwest.

"Matt, I have little idea of who these healers are and what all these sessions are going to be about, but you have to learn about the chakras or at least the pineal gland." Peter said to Matt on the flight to Vancouver.

Matt skeptically half listened. He thought he was just along for the adventure.

Once in Vancouver, Pat Bermel and his company ran the production and the brothers had little to do. The pilot filming introduced them to basically every "mainstream new age" treatment and energy work. All of these healers were brought together by the spirit of Peter's idea and Pat's connections to the super-charged owner of the crystal shop where the filming was held.

When Peter relayed his impressions to me, he said "I loved all of them instantly. I had no idea of their techniques. It all was brand new to me, yet all of it and their spirits and energies resonated within me completely. There was something calming, exciting and familiar about each of them. I felt like I was home. Coupled with the beauty and a sensation that something magical was happening in that spirit-charged Pacific Northwest, I was transformed." Peter purged again.

The premise of the pilot was for sessions to be filmed, then the healers and the "patients" would talk on camera about the session after completion.

It was now Peter's turn and he was still skeptical of all these new aged activities. The healer first performed a guiding saint reading. It didn't really mean much to him to look at the picture on a card and learn that the saint depicted was his guide.

Next was a chakra meditation and Peter remembered thinking, as she guided his attention up the back of his spine, "This isn't working. Nothing is happening. This whole thing is a big con, and I am going to have to go out and get filmed lying about how great it is."

"And now the heart chakra and then to the throat," the healer continued to guide him.

Peter internally thinks, "... still nothing...what a fraud it all is, this whole trip, the project— This whole project is a big lie!"

"Next I want you to focus on your pineal gland," the healer said.

Suddenly from the floor he felt a wave of energy rise through his toes and rush up all of his body to his head. He had the sensation of floating off the chair.

"My whole body warmed and I felt myself lifting over the scene." Peter dumbfoundingly exclaimed.

This was the birth of his ongoing and expanding magical life. May 2, 2011. A mystical moment that ignited an unique and powerful spirit. A complete stranger to me then, but in a few days Peter was going to have a profound effect on the course of my life. .

The filming was over, so Matt and Peter planned to spend the night at Whistler. Matt had struck up a conversation with one of the healers named, Yoko Haga. She had mentioned there was a special meeting of biodynamic farming leaders taking place in Squamish. On the way to Whistler, with both of them feeling elevated by the odd experiences with the pilot shoot, they noticed a sign for the farm.

"Let's go to that meeting," said a revived Matt. He too had picked up the power of the healers and the energy of the Northwest. While he remained a skeptic, he had coined the trip with a question, "Can the world really be this magical?" And upon his return to Minneapolis he had crows seemingly following him for over a year.

Peter, who was no longer Peter, surprised himself with an agreeing response free from his usual reluctance. "Let's go check out that farm."

The largest hummingbird they both had ever seen greeted them as the bird cut the silence and buzzed by their ears. Startling them both.

As if on cue, Ferdinand Vondruska, the owner of the farm appeared and welcomed them into the circle of the meeting on biodynamic farming. A subject neither knew, but being invited into a powerful circle somehow added more confirmation that Shifting Circles was on the right track and deep forces were in play in the Pacific Northwest.

After the meeting they told Yoko about the hummingbird that welcomed them. She said it was her spirit animal and showed her hummingbird earrings. Matt and Peter thought of the timing, size and force of that humming bird and this magical Yoko Haga and the whole day with the healers. They felt drugged with excitement and wonder.

The next day, back in Chicago, Peter received a phone call from a friend of one of the healers from Shifting Circles. She said she was connected to a woman that annually visited the Altai Mountains in Russia and did energy work and was seeking to tap into the Akashic Record. She had heard about Shifting Circles from her friend and they agreed it would be a great experience if Shifting Circles could come with them and document their energy work in The Altai.

Four days prior, a discussion like that would have seemed absolutely ridiculous and beyond his ability to even imagine. He hadn't even heard of the Altai or, for that matter the Akashic Record....other than some faint memory connected to Genghis Khan.

Yet, as he hung up the phone, the momentum, buzz and new spirit energies from Vancouver were still strongly percolating in him and his new heart spoke, "The Altai? I know nothing of it, but this is possible. Somehow going to Altai is possible."

Immediately after he hung up, he was out of his building to meet his best friend in Chicago. His friend wanted to hear about the pilot and Vancouver and everything. It would take hours of walking and talking to even try to sort out the magical weekend and now he had the Altai on his mind as well to keep the circle rippling. The world was alive and spinning through him in some way completely foreign and exciting. Where would this all take him and what of the fascinating healing energy he felt certain to meet?

What do you ponder?

Chapter 5

Parallel Dimensions Converge

My life had settled down a little after that amazing start to 2011. May was upon me and I went to Chicago to visit my Dad. He was an avid gambler and loved The Kentucky Derby. Derby Day is the first Saturday in May, and this year it also happened to be my birthday. The plan was to drive from Chicago to Churchill Downs, the home of the Derby. We had done this trip before when I was in high school, but since we lived in Seattle, we had flown to St. Louis and drove to the Derby. Spending a long weekend in Chicago and Kentuckiana sounded fun and a good distraction from the mess of my new apartment.

Ode to the Kentucky Derby

Heading down, crossing the Mustatuck,

It looks like muck.

Then Tippecanoe River next,

Who came up with that text?

Chairs in the streets,

Everyone grooving to beats.

Hats, hats…everywhere hats,

Mint juleps until I'm seeing bats.

Same guy, different cigar,

Oh Kentucky, I wonder where I are.

Horses join the party,

I place a bet and yell "Go Hardy!"

A day ingrained in my mind,

Everyone in the South is so kind.

Back in Chicago after the Derby, I went on a long walk. My Dad was at work and I was flying home the next day. I walked through Lincoln Park wearing my new favorite purple T-shirt I had just gotten in Vancouver, BC the week before.

I was following no path in particular, but when I saw Lincoln Park, I was attracted to it's nature...knowing there would probably be a few good bird poop shapes. My Splat Story had become quite a hit with my kids and friends and I self-published a simple copy of the book. I made "Splat" stickers and created a website. It was an entertaining and light-hearted story that made me happy.

As I entered the park, I saw two tall, strikingly good-looking men talking and smiling, walking in the opposite direction I was going. I paid no attention other than I noticed them because of their handsome features and they were smiling. I was also smiling with Splat on my mind and continued my aimless walking, always looking for a sign.

Dream

A million miles away and still detectable.

Standing on the ground,

A star in the sky invites a dream.

It takes optimism to make that dream attainable.

Wish upon a star and dream big

Your dream could affect the rest of your journey.

The events of the last couple of months had ignited me beyond bird poop. My wandering mind in Chicago was going through a daydream of a communal utopia, living off unencumbered land, fully sustainable with wind powered turbines….wandering….

I let my mind slip back to my childhood and into Yam's bedroom. A terrible summer storm was beating against her window. We looked at Babar, the Elephant dimly lit by our glow worms. The animals were speaking to us again. A conversation in a language of subtleties that all living creatures can hear.

REVERBERATION 2

Holographic Universe

Yam and I have what we call "prizm vision" and are a set of a "chosen few." ARG enters from another dimension through the wall. ARG is the Alien Robot God we made up in our art class.

ARG tells us, "you can see the spectrum. But being chosen does not mean you can carry out the message. It takes a lifetime of compassion, determination, kindness. A yearning of mental aptitude in order to be released from the mundane toil. If you desire only the purest of intentions, you will be granted a hidden wealth." Yam looks at me, me at her. Did our imaginations just run wild??

ARG speaks again, "Listen, my children. Do you hear the wind? Do you hear the words whispered by these ancient trees? This is the universal language of subtleties. All species understand this language, but not everyone hears it. Imagine how a dog senses your fear. We live in a holographic universe. Earth is not the only home. You children have laid in ARG's bed of enlightenment and ARG will forever be with you. ARG is powerful and infinite."

Alien Robot God has three parts: The first part (Alien) is the out-of-your-world events that are unexplainable, but true. The "magic" creatively powers ingenuity. The second part is the strength of a robot. Your commitments are met by driving your actions and completing the every day minutiae that must be done. The third power is found in earthly crystals: Positive energy...it is the metaphysical, spiritual side that one only knows within themselves. Once enlightened, you can see ARG in others. With a perfect balance of ARG, It is a prizm of a universe, there is universal peace, love and harmony. Time is inevitable and unavoidable. As much good as for evil, but change is truly the only constant in this life. ARG is beautiful. She transcends gender, race and age. Freedom from toil can exist by following your signs. Making steps in the right direction, but I caution you: a symbol is not more important than the flow of time & the underlying continuity of experience. Collective thought holds infinite genius. Tap into that genius to spread the message. Conquer fear and live inspired. ARG only chooses the finest of messengers and I know you two are some of our finest."

END REVERBERATION

Cradled by Chaos

Goofy & serious;

Happy, yet confused.

Thoughtful but forgetful;

Smart, lacking common sense.

Its maddening calmness,

agitated stillness.

This was such a beautiful day in Lincoln Park. I had been walking for hours and was just emerging on the Gold Coast side of the park, walking down State Street. I looked up and those two good-looking men I had seen hours earlier were walking towards me again...Impossible. A city of how many? And I cross paths with these two men twice in one day? They, too, have the power of ARG I tell myself.

They smile at me and I at them, again. As we walk past each other, I can't help myself. I remembered the regret of not talking with my future self in the grocery store during that synchronicity, and sometimes universes only collide once. Here he was a second time. ....so I kinda laughed and said, "hey, didn't I see you today? Like, hours ago on the other side of the park?"

It is Peter.

They both laugh and Peter says, "Is that shirt from Vancouver, BC? I was there just yesterday with my brother shooting a pilot to a TV show about energy workers. It's called Shifting Circles."

I'm flabbergasted and say, "Yeah, I was there last week. I've been writing a kids book about a bird who poops art and I just go wherever the day takes me."

Peter, bald headed and rather regal looking said he would like to check out my book. I did have a Splat business card with my new website on it and I gave him one. He looks at the name on my card and he says, "Huh, Krystal Kelley, of course, the girl with the hummingbird tattoo.. I'm Peter, this is my friend Mitchell."

I didn't catch the hummingbird connection until much later, but we were somehow instant friends. Right there, standing on State Street in Chicago, Illinois the day before my birthday, he tells me, "We shot a pilot for a tv show about energy workers. I just got off the phone with a woman who told me there is a group planning to open an energy portal in order to reground Mother Earth and unlock her ancient wisdom. They are going to the Altai Mountains in Siberia in August to do this major energy work for Mother Earth and they want our show to go with them."

I'm floored...I don't know why, but I said, "I need to go with them."

"The leader has been preparing for this trip for over ten years because of a premonition she had decades ago. Since then, there are about a dozen people who have been planning to join her. I also know there are a group of shamans from Columbia that are going, a Siberian shaman and a Navajo wisdom-keeper along with other energy workers. Most of them come from Seattle, that is where the organizer, Carol lives."

I just stand there, still on State Street in Chicago, IL staring at these two new friends. I push Peter in the arm and say, "Peter, I live in Seattle!! I fly back tomorrow. I feel like I have to go on this trip, can you please email me Carol's contact information?"

"Listen Krystal, I don't know why, but this is too much of a coincidence. You do have to go. Something sent me to send you," Peter said. His newly discovered connection to his spirit messaging had just said Shifting Circles could somehow go to the Alltai. It came true in about two hours: Krystal Kelley is a part of Shifting Circles, the girl with the hummingbird tattoo.

How stunned Peter must have felt. In a few months he had started following a path of synchronicity and connections to the creation of a spiritually transforming TV pilot. Then upon a day after his return to Chicago, he met and guided me in the direction of the Altai. Nearly ten years later, it continues to be a head shaking and exciting day for both of us.

Having gone so far out, we go in.

Chapter 6

Preparing for the Inner Realm

We walk off in different directions, but our minds are connected in the same dimension. My head is spinning. In three short months I am heading to Siberia! I haven't been more excited or felt more called to do anything in my life. A most remarkable connection of events and destiny.

The **Altai Mountains**₁ are considered by the local indigenous people to be the navel of Mother Earth. A major energy point on the planet, the mountain range has been the spiritual retreat dating back 40,000 years. It's a very remote area; the borders of modern day Russia, China, Mongolia, Uzbekistan and Kazakhstan meet in the Altai Mountains. I later found out that in many South American tribes AND the local Altai tribe have the same legend!

The legends surmised say: One day, Mother Earth would be out of balance and spinning out of control. The Condor from the South would meet the Eagle from the North at the naval to restore the heart of the planet. This group of energy workers were bringing the Shaman from South America to meet with the Eagle of Altai in the North. The local Altai people consider themselves to be the Eagle.

There was no doubt in my mind that I was supposed to be there...to tell the story, to be a bridge, to help ground Earth's energy field and to radiate that energy with my "crystal pen." The very pen that connects all my lives, creates prizms of rainbows into the future.

After leaving Peter and Mitchell, I was pulled to walk into a Barnes & Noble store. I was so completely sure I am going on this journey that I bought a red Moleskin journal to begin to document this amazing journey. I named it, "A Vessel for the Message."

I flew back home and could NOT WAIT to see the girls. My daughters were on break from school and they got to come to my new apartment for a full week. It was the first time they were seeing their new room and I couldn't be more excited! They arrived and of course, I had no food in the house and the girls were hungry. I didn't have a TV yet, so I set up my laptop for them to watch a movie. I ordered takeout from the Thai restaurant across the street. As I run back from the restaurant, it was pouring buckets of rain, I glanced up to the balcony above mine. Two little girls looking like the EXACT same age as my daughters are standing there watching me get drenched.

"Hi, I'm Apple, this is my sister Caryn" the older one says, shockingly sounding mature for her age.

"Hey, how old are you?" I ask.

They tell me what I already know and I say to them, "I have two daughters your age, do you want to come play?"

"Daaaad!!!" They yell inside.

Their Dad pops his head out of the sliding door along with a huge cloud of black smoke. At this point I'm wondering what in the heck is going on in that apartment??

"Do you mind if we all come down to play?" he laughs. "I just tried to start a fire in our fireplace, but the chimney flue was closed, so I smoked us out of here."

I laugh and say of course.

The girls were instant BFF's and played all evening dressing up with my clothes and high heels while Carl and I chatted.

"So, what's your deal?" Carl asks and adds, "I moved in a few weeks ago, but I never see you here."

"Yeah, I kinda go where the day takes me. I was in Vancouver BC, then went to Chicago and the Kentucky Derby with my Dad, and now I'm planning a really big trip to Siberia to do some energy work with Indigenous people there. I'm writing a book."

Carl tells me he has traveled all over the world touring with a music band and that he is opening a restaurant on the corner. We have a lot in common, I love talking business and I explain how I'm trying to sell my coffee shop that I own. I can already tell he and his girls are lifelong friends.

Spring

The water feels thicker….percolating.

Drip, drip, drip.

Each drip brings purity;

My mind, the filter.

The dark course grounds of my memory,

Recycled into my garden;

Fertilizing future growth and richer soil.

A thought ephemerally grown in the mind,

Once written lasts into eternity.

Like a photo of an evanescent flower,
to relish and share until….

Infinity!

The girls go back to school and I'm feeling sad that they are finishing the school year in Westport, so Kate and two of her brothers (she has seven) take me out to cheer me up. We go to the local Irish Pub near my brother's house.

My brother shows up for a while and shows us a funny video he took. It was a lady in business clothes walking down the street. She looked totally normal except that she had one shoe on and one bare foot. She wasn't carrying the other shoe in her hand, just walking as if nothing was strange. We watched the video a million times and laughed harder each time…sometimes, it's just the little things that can cheer you up.

My brother left and we were still laughing and telling stories at closing time. Kate's sister-in-law worked at the pub since Kate knows everyone, the cook joined us as the restaurant was closing and we went to Karaoke. The cook was quiet, but intriguing and it got pretty instant between us. I didn't catch his name though.

Days and nights seem to melt together, I'm getting prepared for my trip to Siberia. I'll be gone for a month. It's a long time to be away from the kids, especially since I was already gone during half of their school year. I know this trip is a part of a whole, the time away will seem insignificant in the future, yet my ingredient is a part of the recipe swimming around in a briny tin can. I have to carry out this mission.

I start learning more about what this mission is meaning to everyone involved. There is a woman in Seattle, Karah, who has organized grounding groups all over the planet to meditate on August 11th when we will be in Altai. I find out that there are several million people who are going to participate. I visit with Karah at her home in North Seattle to learn more. She tells me about the Columbian Shamans who have a mission tied into

Karah's grounding ceremonies. The Shamans are from the Sierra Nevada de Santa Marta Mountains on the Caribbean coast of Colombia. They live in sacred ancestral lands of four Indigenous Peoples: the Kogi, Arhuaco, Wiwa, and Kankuamo. It is the world's tallest coastal mountain range, containing nearly every ecosystem on the planet: glaciers, tundra, alpine lakes, deserts, rainforests, wetlands, and coral reefs. They believe it is the heart of the planet.

These peoples are direct descendants of an ancient civilization known as the Tayrona, they all speak distinct languages but share the belief that they are the guardians of the heart of the world. Karah explained to me that they believe that if they leave their island, the planet's heart will stop beating. But, some of the Kogi Mamos had a dream that they must go to the navel of the planet. In 2,000 years of lineage, this particular group had never left the island, needless to say, leaving their homeland and traveling all the way across the globe is a BIG mission. They felt called to Altai, so they were trekking with our group.

I really like Karah, she studied acupuncture and chinese herbs yet she used to be a welder. My kind of a badass lady. I was a little disappointed she wasn't coming on the trip with us, but I understood the importance of her grounding work in Seattle. I was grateful for the comfort it gave me knowing I'll be so far away from home.

I visited the Russian Embassy in Downtown Seattle to obtain a Visa I need to travel within Russia. There are so many borders in Altai, yet it is one land. All this red tape is bullshit and just another part of the "politricks" I can't stand.

I think about Yam, my childhood friend. She isn't talking to me anymore. Just before I left my husband, she came to visit us in Westport. She was living in the other Washington, Washington DC. She and I had hinged different directions after college. I took the hippy dippy route and danced through life trying broadcast media, real estate, starting and subsequently selling a few businesses. Yam held more degrees than businesses I had sold. She went to Princeton, then Yale and became an international attorney. I liked to think that she was infiltrating the "politricks" from the inside, casting ARG's mission of love, compassion and ethos on all the evil systems. But, that was my childhood imagination, Yam was getting married as I was getting divorced. Evil imploded as goodness exploded and simultaneously, we didn't talk. Deep down, I'm not too worried about it though. I know one day she will become President of the United States. She will need a close advisor and someone to talk to the

Aliens. I'm pretty sure I'll be her first call. I'll work at the Whitehouse with her and we can catch up then.

Right now, I have a world to save.

Carl has the opening to his restaurant and Kate and I go. I keep meeting random people who have been to Siberia. Someone at the restaurant went to Siberia for a kettlebell competition. He told me to bring instant coffee.

Good GAWD am I glad I met him! If I don't get my coffee, the world will literally end. I add instant coffee to my expanding packing list.

Speaking of coffee, my favorite barista gives me his pocket knife for good luck, "in case I need it to slay a Siberian tiger." That's exactly why he is my favorite barista, his dramatic flair is as refreshing as his coffee.

My days are filled with tasks for the trip. I have friends who contact me to bring rocks and crystals, deeply personal items that they want me to bring to Altai to recharge them. My heart grows thinking how much this trip means not only to me, but to so many people.

My nights are filled with that cook Kate knew. He does have a name and he has me twitterpated. For once, Kate writes ME a poem.

JASON

Out of the norm…

People think they know.

Not the usual suspect,

The unspeakable speaks for itself.

The ebb and flow seems to work…

Maybe better than it should.

No pretensions, no predictions

Let's just live in the moment.

Enjoy what is…

One day at a time

Feeling what just being here gives.

It was the 4th of July and Carol called from Russia. Carol is our trip's organizer and she was there a month ahead of everyone else. I could sense stress in her voice. We didn't have much time to connect between our first meeting and her leaving for Russia. It was all very rushed. I was the very last trekker to join the group. In fact, I got my visa application to the Russian Embassy on the last day it was allowed in order to travel for the dates that we were going.

Carol is concerned that the 5th dimensional energy at Altai will be too much for me. She clearly doesn't understand the synchronicities that have brought me to join her. I assure her everything will be just fine.

I explain to her, "The inner realm is not only real, it supersedes western mindsets. A revelation can be felt where there are no boundaries. The intersection of indigenous culture and western culture is a balance. This intersection is not like a road, rather more like an estuary where freshwater and saltwater intermingle. There is a paradox in this estuary where extreme care is necessary for us to stay warm in our hearts. I'm coming along as a bridge with pure, positive energy."

She feels relieved that she called and we look forward to seeing each other in a month.

It's free Slurpee day, so I take my girls and Apple and Caryn to get Slurpees. They sure are BFF's. We make up some new words:

Somewhen—to relate "some" with time instead of place like "somewhere"

Rememorable—to remember memories

Supernal – super nocturnal

Mellow hardcore—self explanatory, no definition needed.

Nithing—similar to "nothing," but with more emphasis. You must say it like you are Russian, wrinkle your nose and say it with disgust, "Nithing!"

Kids are silly and we all laugh. Carl reminds me to pack super glue and duct tape. Good idea!

Carol called again. I was still in bed, she was worried because my name was not on the border permit list when she passed through Tyungar today. She tells me Jackie is going to try to help when she gets to Moscow to clear up the confusion.

I call Maia, one of the trekkers from Seattle, who has been to Altai ten years before. Maia is the one who I'll be flying with. She assures me everything will be okay. I feel as if my path might not be the same as the group's. It's okay, I'm not discouraged or worried.

Besides, in the meantime, I really like the energy I have with Jason. It seems easy, free of angst or competition… like life is a collaboration. He is also very supportive of my trip. He was in the Navy and had two deployments to the Middle East. He understands when you feel you have a duty larger than life, you must go.

I light a candle that night and place it in front of my Buddha statue, "Let this flame light my way through dark borders."

Supernal Encounter

Just a dude with a name I can't recall,

A mysterious presence and all.

Sure of the thoughts in his head,

Overly good in bed.

Now he enters my dream without a scream.

Creative,

Open heart,

Not looking for a part.

Respectability

And confident,

Different.

Nothing is easy;

Invariability is the constant…

Verses sung with intent.

Enterprising,

NOT intimidated AND

Surprising.

Days and nights are spinning together. I have most of my packing gathered but not I'm not fucking organized… it was a list and now is a pile on my floor. I need help packing but I go get a tattoo instead. I tattoo "promise" on my pinky finger. It's my promise to my girls to come home. They are feeling sad that I'm leaving.

I go to the courthouse to file divorce papers, I sign my name and date July 25th. Well, that's ironic…that's the same day I got married. I laugh at how coincidence follows me around like a good friend. I do the math and realize it has been 13 years; lucky 13 I guess! I go back to my apartment and bake a berry cobbler for the girls.

I believe there is a real reason I'm heading to Siberia…I've been working towards this my entire life.

REVERBERATION 3

My Energy Field

I remember a trip I took to Arizona in college. My grandparents were living in Scottsdale and my mom was going to fly down to meet me there. We were going to go to the Grand Canyon on a senior citizen bus tour.

I arrived a few days before my mom and decided I wanted to drive to Peoria where Spring Training was taking place. I wanted to watch the Mariners play baseball. I was working at the time in TV News & Sports and one of my freelance gigs was to produce the "Diamond Vision" at the Mariner's home games. I spent a lot of time at the stadium and was a big M's fan. I borrowed my Grandpa's green 1968 Rambler. I awoke before the sun and Grandpa made me fresh squeezed orange juice. He gave me a map and the keys and told me to have fun. I didn't have tickets to the game but I was hoping my press pass from Seattle would give me admission.

The orange juice was more refreshing than coffee, so I set out driving down a long, extremely flat road. There were no street lights and the dim headlights made it hard to see. I thought to myself, "At least I can't get lost on roads like these."

At that moment, the brightest light I've ever seen flashed to my left. It flashed so fast that I thought if I had blinked I would have missed it. But, I didn't blink and honest to ARG, the next thing I remember I am standing in Peoria at the M's game. I have no recollection how I got there.

I hear someone calling my name, "Krustal!!! Hey Krust!"

Ok, ok, don't laugh, my nickname in high school was "Krust."

I turned around to see two really good friends from high school. Jeff's dad was a pilot, so they flew down for free from Seattle. The best part is that they had an extra ticket to the game. One of their friends had bailed at the last minute, so we sat in the outfield, watched the game and got sunburnt to a crisp with the Arizona sun baking our Seattle skin. They had a hotel near the stadium and I stayed the night with them swimming under the stars. It was only then that I remembered that light. I didn't mention it though. I had no words to describe what I had seen or what had happened, plus I was super happy to have bumped into these guys and spend the day with them.

Is that when the alignment happened? The pure light to my dreams, intuition and coincidence... Or was it those late night sleepovers with Yam? Maybe it all started BEFORE I was born...the premonition my mom had five years before she birthed me, the day she met my dad, she saw them holding a baby in a doorway. She was 12 years old. No one has thoughts of a baby when they are 12, but this wasn't a thought, it was a vision, its an energy field around me.

END REVERBERATION

Chapter 7

International Altai Expedition

Unfortunately, I don't think my energy field alone is going to pack my bags for Siberia. Along with the usual items, I was bringing along audio and video equipment to document the trip for Shifting Circles. I was going back to my TV production roots, but this was different. When I worked in TV, I was on a production TEAM. There were many of us working on the show. This would be a solo adventure with me trying to wear many hats at once. Technology had made gear much smaller and portable, so I thought I could do it.

I prep (or procrastinated) for the trip by reading through Carol's blog about our "Altai Fellowship 2011 International Expedition" as she has named it. Carol wrote:

"What Is the Altai "High Vibrational Energy Field"?

Please excuse my terminologies and translate them as well as you can into your own understanding. English is not suited to conveying spiritual information, so I am compelled to use a series of metaphors, so rather than looking for a literal understanding, note instead how you feel when you read this material. That will give you the most accurate understanding of what I'm trying to convey.

Tuning into the Altai Frequency

Our human senses are similar to radio channels — touch is a soft rock station, sight is a jazz station, etc. Our perception is a narrow band in a very broad spectrum of vibrational frequencies. Humanity as a whole has been tuned into a "material" network, with very limited awareness of other vibrations.

The transition that is now being so widely discussed globally is apparently the culmination of natural galactic cycles, with the result being an expansion of human consciousness after a period of chaos. While tuned into our "material" network, we have collectively forgotten that there is no such thing as separation. We have been operating under the illusion that we are independent beings, rather than integral parts of an awesomely complex and completely inclusive system that goes by the names of "live," "love," and "Oneness." Fortunately, through the ages there have been a few people who have been able to maintain at least some awareness of the larger system. These are our shamans, seers, oracles, prophets, mystics, and sacred fools. Indigenous cultures that have maintained the concept of "power with" have maintained deeper awareness than Western cultures that have adopted "power over" concepts. Even so, the links have been tenuous, and have been maintained with great sacrifice.

The protection of Shambhala

Apparently, all previous attempts to navigate through the chaos have failed, with references to the destruction of Atlantis, extinguished life on Mars, and the explosion of the Planet Maldek into the asteroid belt. This time, however, we seem to be coming through.

Many shamans and mystics have understood through their awareness that at some point in Earth's history, humanoids of some sort were fully aware. According to my guidance from Spirit, there was a great spiritually-based civilization in Central Asia, during a time when the Xingjiang Plateau of western China was a great sea. When humanity cycled into its current "materialistic" way of being, the enlightened beings were no longer generally accessible to humanity. In other words, the access portal was closed to us. In connecting the bits of information I receive, I understand that this civilization was Shambhala.

However, in the great mountain ranges that surround this former sea — the Himalayas, Tienshan, and Altai/ Sayan — there are places where the gate or veil is thin and the immense energies of life flow freely. In these places, the enlightened beings appear to people as luminous, white, glowing Light Beings. The Altai Range in southern Siberia is such a place, so much so that a whole body of knowledge called the "White Religion" has evolved around people's encounters with these beings, even to the present day. In fact, it was these Light Beings who came to me in a dream in 1998 and asked that I come to Altai. I thought I was imagining things, of course, although the sensation that came with the invitation was so powerful that I did go, and was amazed to find the traditions alive and well there.

The Challenges of the Altai Journey

Altai is not an easy gig. It was, at the time, days by car and train from the nearest airport, and the sacred places could only be accessed after more days on foot or horseback. Weather is unpredictable, and snow in July is not uncommon. But the most difficult aspect, which is so common that the locals joke about it, is that whatever traumas we have buried in our beings — physical, emotional, mental — get triggered. The effect of a trauma is to block the energy flow, and in the presence of the extraordinary flow of energy through Altai, our blockages re-surface painfully. At that point, we have a choice: 1) to project the pain onto whoever is nearby and blame them (causing monumental arguments), or 2) to own the pain and release it, thus healing it.

Because the flow of "life" force is so strong in the Altai area, Altai shamans are renowned for their power. Western technology has finally advanced to the point that it can actually measure this flow, vindicating what the shamans have been saying. Unfortunately, until now, Western scientists have not extrapolated this into a vindication of the truth of the remainder of shamanistic experience — that everything is alive and connected.

Expanded Consciousness

But as we approach the cyclic transition to expanded human consciousness, more and more people have been able to directly access this flow. We understand that humanity has reached a tipping point, at which general access to expanded consciousness will once more be accessible. This is what we are calling the opening of the gate, and the purpose of the Altai Fellowship is to "midwife" this rebirth by actively transmitting the energy out into human consciousness, beginning on August 13, 2011 and actively continuing for a week. The amount of flow, however, depends on the energy then being grounded into the Earth. similar to an electrical system.

Thus, we are calling on people around the world to ground this energy. The personal effect of participating in this grounding is that one's own energy blockages will be cleared and access to expanded awareness

will be enhanced. And this effect is amplified if done in groups.

Blessings all!

I finish reading....Holy Shit! It hits me hard: I leave tomorrow. I say goodbye to my daughters. I tell them I'll visit them in their dreams and I'll be home sooner than they think.

I finish packing at 12:30am. Jason really helps me with my video equipment and my mental state. I'm really lucky I met him, we have a sweet romance for sure. I look forward to spending some more time with him when I get home.

We wake up at 4am, Jason loads my car with my backpack and duffle bag. The duffle bag is full of freeze-dried MRI's that will be consumed on the trek. We go pick up Maia. At one point, she locks herself out of her apartment building when she was taking her bags outside. We have to wake up a neighbor to let us in to get the rest of her bags. This is pure craziness already...but Moscow, here we come!

The flight is long but I'm so exhausted, I fall asleep drooling before we even take off. I wake up mid-air and watch The Devil Wears Prada. It is the only movie that wasn't in Russian aboard our Aeroflot flight. I try to sleep after the movie, but my eyes are burning. There was so much energy going into the preparation for the trip that it has finally hit me I'm on my way. I just sit there crying silently in the dark. I'm going to a country very foreign to me, it feels as if I might as well be headed to the Moon. Their language sounds intimidating as I hear people chatting in Russian all around me on the flight.

I started thinking about how sad my daughters were, but how strong they were when they said goodbye…I'm also realizing I have some real feelings for Jason; the guy who I didn't even know his name just a few months ago. How can love happen so fast? I genuinely care for him and his future. Then, I think of all the wonderful people who helped me prepare for this trip. All the little things add up to a huge web of love and support. I feel super special. I believe that even from thousands of miles away, in Altai, that web will be my cocoon. I can be a beautiful butterfly that hatches to fly weightlessly and brighten the day. Kinda like the feeling that YouTube hippy got when he saw a double rainbow—he laughed, he cried: pure joy.

If I can make a difference in perspective for someone, with my Splat art…the ability to see beauty in anything, even bird poop, maybe I can spread love and laughter with my stories.

I write in my journal some new story ideas for a second book of Splat.

We have a long lay-over in Moscow. Over 24 hours. I convince Maia to venture out of the airport with me. She is reluctant because she is worried we will lose our way and miss our flight to Novisibirsk. We put our luggage in a locker and got on the Subway.

I quickly realize the Cyrillic alphabet makes it very hard to find our way to Red Square. I copy the signs we are passing by writing in my journal letter for cyrillic letter where we have been. We were going in literal circles around Moscow. The subway is not in a grid....it's designed in a circle and spreads almost like a spider web around the city. We are misdirected by a handsome Russian who speaks English. We don't find Red Square and decide to head back to the airport so we won't miss our flight.

At least the people-watching in Moscow was fun. Women love their tight pants and heels, even on the cobblestone streets. They also have massive purses with flashy things hanging off them. Their purses reminded me of my middle school backpack that had all sorts of buttons and keychains obnoxiously hanging off it.

We stopped at a Starbucks in Moscow. It seems like a safe place to use the bathroom. Men in business suits order a shot of vodka and a shot of coffee. The barista sets it on the bar and the men take each shot and walk out.

Interesting way to drink coffee. Most of the public spaces smelled like stale vodka and body odor.

I learn more about Maia as well. This is her second trip to Altai. She is what I would describe as an empath. She has significant psychic abilities, she is telepathic and is able to do remote viewing. Maia had a strong **premonition**₂ before this trip. She is also highly sensitive to loud noises and other vibrational currencies.

We land in Novosibirsk. We stumble off the plane, my pack feels heavy and the duffle bag of food is such a ball and chain to carry. I see this young woman with a beautiful moon-shaped face, she is running towards us. She is smiling really big and has her hands out ready to give us a big hug. Refreshingly, she speaks English.

"You must be Maia and Krystal. I'm SO happy to see you." She gives us the biggest hug.

"I'm Luna, Svetlana's daughter. I'll be your translator and guide to Altai." I already love Luna, she has such wonderful energy.

Luna and her family are from The Altai Republic, whose people are Central Asian. After the break-up of the Soviet Union, the Altai Republic became part of Russia.

I feel a huge sigh of relief getting the warm welcome from Luna. We chatted all the way to Lyuda's house. We are staying there for a night before a long overnight train ride on the Trans-Siberian Railroad.

We learn that Novisibirsk is home to the Ob River, one of the only rivers that flows North in the world. The other river that flows North is the Nile River in Africa.

Novisibirsk is also the fastest growing city in the world. It's largely due to a controversial pipeline that they are laying through Siberian mountain ranges. The work is disturbing wildlife, but it will be able to deliver fuel across a vast continent. Clearly, money is the goal but environmentalists are not happy and neither are the indigenous people. Luna's family is indigenous to the Altai Mountains and that is where she grew up. She is living in Novosibirsk finishing up her business and language studies at the University. She is delightful to chat with and we have a lot in common.

Driving to Lyuda's apartment building, I noticed Novosibirsk's urban landscape was polarized: brutalist architectural buildings strikingly juxtaposed with traditional Russian architecture. Lyuda's building looks like most of the brutalist buildings--a large concrete structure with tiny windows and barely any doors. In my opinion, it looked like a prison or a barrack. The elevator was so tiny, only one person could load at a time with their bags. We took turns getting to the 8th floor.

Lyuda was in her 70's if I had to guess and was extremely kind. She only spoke Russian, so Luna did her best to keep up with the translating. Lyuda had a lot to say, but I feel like a lot of it was lost in translation.

Another trekker, Carolyn joins us. She lives in the Methow Valley in Washington and had also participated in the 2007 trek with Maia and Carol. Carolyn, Luna and I go see a Railway Workers Art Exhibit while Maia napped.

Upon returning to Lyuda's, we are served tomatoes and nasturtium leaves. I had never eaten a nasturtium leaf, but I liked it…it tasted like a spicy lettuce. Both were from her garden, but I wasn't really sure where that garden was in this nearly windowless apartment. I learned that most urban Russians have country homes with gardens called "dachas". 80% of the produce grown in Siberia is grown in these private gardens.

Lyuda says she works 3 jobs. All are special projects. The description of her work is extremely vague, but she complains about the inefficiencies of her government. Oh, I wish I understood Russian…I feel like I was missing some juicy details. We found out that one of the women who was supposed to trek with us couldn't make it. Her life was being threatened somehow.

Oh my ARG, what have I gotten myself into??

I notice a college-assignment-looking-text-paper stapled together on the side table of the room that Maia and I are sharing. Luna is sleeping on the couch, Carolyn is on the floor. It's a tiny two bedroom apartment. The paper has a heading in English that reads, "The Fight Against Corruption in the System of the State and Municipal Administration: Lessons Learnt from the Reforms." The paper itself was in Russian and it was written by Carol. I wonder what in the heck it is about?

We spend the evening chatting about conscious language. Luna calls me a "solar seed" and I don't know what that means, but it sounds cool. She also tells us funny things about Russian translation to English like the literal translation of "sunglasses" is "sun insurance glasses". We go to bed early, we are all exhausted.

We take the tiniest taxi to the train station…We sit in silence on the ride, it feels as if there is hardly room for air inside the small hatchback. My mind starts wandering and I am feeling a longing for home. I miss home, the kids…and….Jason. I haven't known him long, but I find myself longing for him.

Maia breaks the silence with a very loud hiccup. It startled her and took her breath away. She looks at me, we are squished up against each other in the back seat.

"What were you thinking about?" she asks me.

"I was thinking that I miss Jason?" I answer in a question because my rational mind is questioning my heart.

"Well, you should follow your heart. Your energy field jumped when you thought about him and that's powerful." Maia explained exactly how I felt. I came to find out that Maia's hiccups have deep significance. She involuntarily hiccups when she is in the vicinity of someone or something that raises the energy. It's like her body is an energy barometer.

We rode the rest of the way to the train station in silence. I was smiling.

Click, clack…sway, sway, the Trans-Siberian train rolled all night. It was a symphony of snores throughout the cabin. Most passengers were lulled to sleep by the gentle rocking. We were traveling to Bisk, Russia, I believe SouthEast from Novisibirsk. During daylight, we saw small towns full of tin roofs with concrete houses that almost looked like shacks. Outside of one of the towns, we traveled for probably 20 minutes seeing only a sea of

69

sunflowers. Yellow flowers deep in the peripheral vision, it was like a beautiful painting with no brushstrokes.

We are on our way to Luna's sister's house in Gorno-Altaysk. Gorno-Altaysk is the capital town of Altai Republic. I'm learning that the locals spell Altai with a 'y', Altay. Gorno-Altaysk is where the Mayma River merges with the Katun River in the foothills of the Altay Mountains.

Gorno-Altaysk shockingly reminds me of the town I lived in throughout high school. When I was in middle school, my parents decided to move from our urban home in Seattle to the foothills of the Cascade Mountains. A little town called Enumclaw, which can be interpreted from the Salish language as the "place of evil spirits." Little did I know that I traveled across two continents to end up in a familiar place. Gorno-Altaysk can be translated to mean "about this sound listen." I felt as if I heard the language of subtleties in the mountains of the North Cascades as deeply as I could hear them in Altay. The reverberations are strong, but I feel a nervous rock at the bottom of my stomach. Something is wrong.

We arrive at Luna's sister's house and Carol has called saying that my border permit is still missing. I started crying, this isn't supposed to happen. Everything was going to work out. Didn't Jackie help in Moscow at the

Embassy? I legitimately feel frightened. What will I do in Siberia alone?? I don't speak Russian!

Luna and Maia instantly start brainstorming. Luna called her mom and she told us to go to an agency in Gorno-Altaysk. Despite the pouring rain, we left on foot to the office. Trudging through the thick mud, I realize that there is no pavement anywhere, all the roads are dirt.

We make it to what looks like an American DOL office. Clerks sitting behind glass panels with only the basic white walls and plastic chairs. Luckily, the Russians were faster than the DOL and we were seen right away. I wasn't noticing any "inefficiencies of government" at this point. Luna booked me as her "guest" for the border tomorrow and I'm feeling much better.

What a whirlwind of emotions! I'm feeling optimistic as we arrive back at the house. Two more trekkers had arrived, Eileen and Patricia. Patricia is from the Navajo Nation and originally grew up in New Mexico, but now lives in Seattle. It was ironic to be meeting her in Altay. I didn't catch much about Eileen. They had been trekking on horseback with the Columbian Shamans, but Patricia had hurt her arm on the horse and Eileen had a wicked cold.

The story of Patricia's horse accident was as scary as it was fascinating. They were trekking on horseback across the

Ukok Plateau, the indigenous name is the "second layer of heaven". Patrician and her horse were near an ancient archeological site. It was where, In 1993, the "Siberian Ice Maiden", an Altai Princess from the 5th century BC was unearthed. It is said that the mummy was so frozen in her tomb that her skin was still pink. Her skin was remarkably preserved with a tattoo of an animal resembling a deer on one of her shoulders and another tattoo on her wrist and shoulders.

The excavation of the Altai Princess is controversial because the local Altai people believe that removing her remains disrupts the natural balance that the Princess is preserving. As Patricia's horse neared the site, it reared up and tried to buck Patricia off. These horses are pack horses and rarely spook. Needless to say, Patricia hurt her arm and decided to re-route their trek and join us.

Eileen and Patricia decided to go to Tyungar, the border tomorrow with us.

Patricia's calm demeanor and intellect were refreshing. We had an evening discussion of the whole and hole of everything human. She explained translations between her Dine language and English. She spoke of a **natural order**3 and exoteric and esoteric living. I had no idea that the Navajo people had such a refined culture. They walk in beauty with Mother Earth and resist most of Western Culture because it is out of balance of a natural way of life.

The next morning, I have a message from Jason and my youngest daughter, Eloise in my email. It was really nice to hear Jason's kind words and he said he misses me. Eloise is having fun at her Gramma's and Sophia, my oldest, is ironically at a sleepover horse camp. My heart feels warm.

We are sitting on a dirt road along the Katun River. I'm with Luna and three women in their 60's, Maia, Patricia, Carolyn and Eileen. I'm watching a black and bright orange butterfly flit across dusty rocks, a grasshopper slowly making its way across the road, narrowly escaping a box truck traveling much too fast for a dirt road. Beautiful, grassy mountains envelope the entire valley. Our driver is a friend of Luna's dad. He too, travels at break-neck speeds down the dusty road past cows, motorized three wheel carts, semi-trucks…it's completely random what we see down the two hours of dirt road. The road is known as the Prison Road. It was laid down over dead prisoner's bodies. Eerily as comforting as the "place of evil spirits." Patricia points out that the word EVIL is the same word in English as LIVE, one is just backwards.

We arrive at the border and wait for at least four hours. It's an armed border. There are guards with large guns on wooden towers and the armed guards on the ground have German Shepherd dogs. There is a small shack with Russian officials inside. Luna tells us all to wait outside. Luckily, the sun is shining and is really warm. At this elevation, it feels like we are closer to the sun than I'm used to. Luna comes back a few times to update us. Maia, Carolyn and Eileen can go across with her, but Patricia and I still have to wait. We wait.

A truck and a bus approach the gate from the opposite direction. They don't seem to have to wait very long on their side. Maybe 15 minutes and they are waived through. We are still waiting. Luna comes outside the guard shack, but isn't coming over to us. It looks like she might cry. She doesn't though.

She talks to the bus driver who was just waved through from the other side. She is writing something on a piece of paper.

Luna is very upset as she approaches us for the last time.

"Patricia and Krystal must go back to my sister's house to wait. They are not letting you through the border today. The bus driver will drop you off at my sister's. She will be expecting you." Luna explains.

I'm surprisingly positive and tell Luna, "We'll meet again!"

She hugs both of us. Patricia and I are off in the direction we came from. Little did I know it would be nearly ten years before I would see Luna again. She will visit me at my home in Seattle shortly after Carol passes away from a brain tumor.

Patricia and I agree that there is something about this situation woven deep into a web of darkness. Patricia explains, "There are endeavors that are incongruent with actions. We seem to be trapped in someone else's web."

I don't have the vocabulary to match Patricia's, but I concur.

Patricia and I arrive very late to Anne's house, it's probably 2am. Anne greets us with big hugs and is crying for joy to see us. The bus driver dropped all the other passengers and then delivered us right to Anne's front door.

We awoke at noon, it was bright and sunny. Anne's house is a typical Siberian home. It has electricity but no indoor plumbing. There is an out-house in the garden and they bring buckets of water into the house to cook with. The house has an exterior wall with siding, then a few feet of space between the interior walls. So, when you look out the window, you are looking through two windows. Apparently, the air between the double walls is better insulation than any material could give them. The heat source is a wood stove in the middle of the house.

Patricia and I wash our clothes in the garden in the sun. It's lovely and comforting to complete a menial task. Patricia continues to tell me about transcendence, a spiraling of upward momentum. I'm in awe of her complex, yet simple thoughts.

Garden Bench

Deep in the mountains of Siberia,

Barking dogs echoes the area.

The sun hot in the sky,

White clouds drift, high and dry.

The wilderness is as wide as deep,

Very few animals dare to creep.

The people carry a permanent poker face,

Literally, they are an amazing race.

They live in harmony, outside of time and space.

We have a lot to learn, it could start
with slowing our pace.

Patricia gets a call that she has a border permit. I bid her farewell...I'm on my own adventure now. Maybe this is what is meant to be, my solitary journey through the Siberian wilderness. I sit in the garden and soak up the sun and brainstorm some options. I think about the motto that got me here: I'll go where the day takes me.

It's a full moon. The day we are supposed to do the ceremony to ground the Earth's energy. I'm not with the group, but I am. I sit in the garden under the bright moonlight. I meditate, I feel really close to ARG and at peace high in the Altai air.

ANOTHER REVERBERATION

One Past Life

I'm transported to another time, another lifetime. I'm Empress Matilda, of the rightful heir to the English Crown. It's around 1120AD. I'm a powerful woman, daughter of King Henry I, granddaughter of William the Conqueror. I became the mother of Henry II. I am the only successor to the throne after the tragic drowning of my brother, William Adelin. My father has faith in my ability to rule, in fact, he makes his court swear on oath that they will uphold this faith after his death.

I am to be the first female monarch to wear the crown. The coronation is only days away. Similar to standing at that Siberian border, I'm living in a web between EVIL and LIVE. The English Church Council is considering a woman "unfit" for the crown. I know I'll be overthrown, but I won't be a martyr. The Council gives the crown to my first cousin, Stephen.

I'm trapped in Oxford Castle in winter. The ice war squeezing me by all sides, I was the center, yet I didn't even feel wet. I sat there, watching the war. I see an escape, in the middle of the night, I flee. Through the frozen River Isis, I avoid capture. I seek refuge in Normandy and look into the grey sky. I am Empress Matilda, I wash my hair. I make a decision not to decide what the outcome will be, I'll let it take shape, just as the ice fjords I crossed.

My claim to the crown is legitimate and I have strong allies. I gather my army and we fight England and King Stephen for ten years. Power will always win over force and we win. Well, sort of.

A stalemate occurs and I negotiate for my son, Henry II to wear the crown. I am Henry II's lead advisor. On my deathbed, I will return again and again to fight for human rights. I am Matilda, Empress of Men AND Women, a powerful, yet little known player in World history and advocate for Women's rights. I become the direct ancestor of the next 24 Monarchs of England, (nearly 500 years) guiding them in my death. It's another 400 years until Queen Mary becomes the actual first woman to wear the crown in 1553. My power, my vision holds steady long after my passing and a true testament that one does not need to be physically present to guide a future.

END REVERBERATION

That future, now, as I sit and meditate as Krystal Kelley, an American mom doing energy work in remote Russia. Where will the next ten years of "battle" take me? I absorb the teachings and loving ways Patricia spoke about and I feel as if I'll intertwine her natural order with my being… ideas start to percolate.

The energy work was intended for Mother Earth, inadvertently, the work occurred inside this Mother. The mother that I am, my core and my gift to the future. I realized the main ingredient is LOVE, not LIVE. We must LOVE instead of LIVE through life. LIVE can too easily become construed as EVIL and incongruencies occur causing torment and unhappiness. My life is most powerful when surrounded by those that inspire me and make my heart feel whole, not those that leave a hole. I will return to Seattle to reverberate this LOVE of life.

Shifting Circles—"becoming what it is" as Peter says.

I land in NYC the day the occupy movement starts. I feel the shift, yet opt to fly straight to Seattle, taking Carl's suggestion and realizing that I would really like to sleep in my own bed. I'm eager to see the kids and Jason and start taking action on my thoughts.

It takes some time to unwind the mind, to release the conditioning that has been taught in this lifetime and through an Akashic record deep in our beings from centuries ago and past lives. We all hold on to emotional trauma that isn't ours. Now, it was the time to stop and "Mind Unwind."

Jason and I conceptualized a space, an art gallery where people could come to have a playground for their creative imaginations. All ages. All welcome. Jason went to art school after being in the Navy and his vision for engaging the creative imagination was as strong as mine. We decided to join forces and we wanted to open a space called "Mind Unwind."

But, where? I looked out the window from my apartment as I was doing the dishes. While I was in Russia, they had burned the house down next door. It was a controlled burn done by the Seattle Fire Department. Everyone in the neighborhood watched and had told me about it when I got home. I looked out my window to see what was going on in the now vacant lot next door. A concrete truck was pulling up and pouring a new foundation. "Hmm, I wonder if they are building our art gallery?" I think jokingly in my head.

As I left my apartment that day, one of the crew was standing on the sidewalk and was stepping out of my way so I could get by.

Instead, I stopped and asked, "Hey, what are they building here?"

He looked at me, and in an ironic (to me) Russian accent said, "You know. A building. You live up there" he pointed towards the sky "and you work down there." He pointed straight ahead at the new imaginary building.

My heart leapt, "Like a live/work??" I asked.

"Ya" he said. "A live work"

I couldn't believe my luck. I knew right then that that building would somehow be mine. I called all my real estate friends who were "in the know". I found the builder and approached him to purchase the building.

Unfortunately, money and timing were not in my favor because of my divorce. I didn't give up. I looked for a friend to buy the building and then I could lease it from them. BINGO! It took a little creativity, but this was a new world for me and I was on a mission to follow my natural order.

Opening Day was electric. It was a moonless sky, the dawn of a new moon. Peter and his brother came from Chicago to help vibrate the energy...and they did! In front of the studio, our friend played an electric guitar. Later in the evening, we had a Mo-town-like band play. Friends, strangers, neighbors all came to celebrate. I had three women (all friends) come in and tell me that they have been praying for something like this to open in this neighborhood for over 7 years...what? People were yearning to spark their creativity whether they knew it or not!

Jason and I formally moved in together upstairs, above the gallery with the kids... we solidified our blended family with a dog. We had a roof deck that had a circular, panoramic view from Mt. Rainier, Cascade Mountains, City Skyline, Olympic Mountains and Elliott Bay. It was unreal and only two blocks from the kids' school.

We curated art exhibits, taught art classes for all ages. We raised the vibration of the entire neighborhood.

Swooping bird is the Dao.

Part II

Tapping into the Natural Order

Spread your wings, the future is as open as the ink on this page. The ability to scribe makes all possibilities infinite. Along with an open heart and open mind, we can accomplish anything we put in front of us. Dedication is the lock, honesty is the key, love is the lubricant.

A new day starts in the middle of the night...does that seem odd that we sleep through the dawn? We awaken to events unfolding. We enter onto the highway of consciousness...the on-ramp traveling half the speed of the highway, entering a new day can be head-spinning. Have you ever entered the highway from a side street? Put the pedal to the metal and jump directly into the human consciousness? Tapping in at the very source puts you ahead of the traffic. Funny to use a "human highway" metaphor for a "natural order" but humans are a part of the natural order and shifting paradigm. Seeing more freely, more of what is there and not what is expected to be there. Releasing expectations and experiences.

Philanthropy and business can be synergetic. Embrace the power of **whole brain thinking,**[4] the comradery of collaborations and feel the electricity that vibrates when new ideas spark.

Matrix & Vibrations

Absorb the energy,

Let your mind be free.

Even if it makes you wanna cry,

Allow the sparks to fly.

Creativity is infinite,

Give it a try, bit by bit.

These words don't belong to me, I am simply using them to process my internal thoughts.

"Fear is the misuse of imagination"—I saw it on Pinterest, who knows who originally said it or thought it? I'm sure hundreds, perhaps thousands of people simultaneously thought it and only a few wrote it down.

Patterns

I notice in retrospect…

A pattern did erect.

What seemed like chaos,

Is a shape I almost lost.

That shape is a sign,

Which repeats, not in a line.

Travelling up, down, right & left,

The sequence gains might.

Thoughts are patterns in your mind. When you start identifying the pattern your mind makes, you can not only interpret the pattern, but you can alter it once you visualize how you want it to look. No first draft is ever good….a mind altered is a mind edited and inspired. An enlightened perspective.

Some see patterns as mathematical, some geometrically, others in color or sound. Patterns can be infinitely measured with multiple layers of shifting brain waves. Perhaps there is an infinite amount of levels and infinite patterns within those levels that create the vast matrix or holographic vortex vacuum. The vacuum of nothingness deep in the base of the mind. Swirling. Black. White. Then hunger overpowers the baseline level. After absolute hunger and nothingness, I go towards compassion for all those who have hungered or are hungry now…for fucks sake…for those who WILL hunger. That compassion grows its own nourishment and you have absolute mental freedom; when you yourself can feed your own hunger, that is creating. You exude energy and you literally vibrate on a different level. Our minds become our wings.

On that shoreline, that stormy shore….I had found a box with my name on it. It contained a fuse that expanded the frequencies of my own mind. Emphasis on expanding to reach new levels. I am able to get to the dimension of time and move freely in it…around the concept of time. I vibrate higher and higher, higher than matter. I learn how to walk through walls. I find it easy to syncopate brain waves with other beings, ARG speaks to me freely. I walk ahead of myself into star-flecked galaxies, endless space. Transported by the speed of thought. I, amongst a distant star, then an earthly shore…it's a liquid, fluid universe.

I stand atop the dune. Tears stream down my face. Not tears of sorrow, but sensitive eyes in the wind. My tongue tastes of briny water, an outburst of joy. I have a sudden realization: I am made of the very ocean that is at my feet and the ocean in front of me is made of me. We are all one. The universe, one salty ambiguous being floating in a sea of black altogether.

The water is thicker now. Thicker than centuries before, as Empress Matilda froze in the dimensional void of her times. She made waves in ice...the unthinkable. We are on the brink of the unthinkable again. Phenomenon, magic, cosmic connections and spirituality are transcending and occupying the universe in a BIG, powerful way. We are essentially transmitters of energy and can tune in and out of different levels of frequency at different times.

Now, we must talk about the mystical change agents. Who are we? Who are they? Or WHAT are we and they?

They and we are the spark, the ignitor, the artist, the composer, the singer, the writer that documents all that happened...that is real, the connections and synchronicities that spawn life. That is the Natural Order.....it is the beginning that has no ending, a transcendent, spiralling dance to this song of life.

Love Life, Live Life, LOVE LIVE LOVE.

Epilogue

wrote this memoir with an important vibrational message: Follow your signs, notice the synchronistic rhythms around you and tap into your inner light to discover your highest potential.

I invite you to continue to follow me through this Shifting Circle (www.shiftingcircles.com) and Post-Corona portal. It's more important than ever to tap into the natural order. There are more portals and more shifting while I document the transcendent travels of me and my growing family...magic and spontaneity to share and inspire.

1. Altai Mountains: Shift of Ages - Altai Frequency by Karah Pino

August, 2011

Mama Mountain.

Mount Belukha rising from the Earth.

Rising like a life-giving breast, source of all beings.

Glacial milk feeding the essence of humanity.

Milked, for love of life,

by conscious intention.

Deep in the heart of the sacred Mt. Beluka in the Altai range lies a triple spiral portal. The triple spiral is a 2-Dimensional interpretation of what is an interdimensional gateway. Through this gateway, life is manifested, grown from seeds of consciousness. Seeds planted within the gateway by intention are in cooperation with Gaia, our loving mother Earth. These seeds germinate in her great belly and manifest through the pathways of minerals and water to the surface of the Earth and flow through mighty rivers across the land and into the great oceans.

The Shift of Ages – Altai Frequency

The shift of ages means many things to many beings. It marks a newly expanded human consciousness that is rising in frequency and capacity. It also marks an awakened Gaia consciousness as our mother Earth awakens to a new stage in evolution. As part of her ascension process, she is shifting many things in her body. She has shut down some portals entirely and in some, she is erasing the imprinting in order to start anew. She is inviting the newly awakened human consciousness to participate in creating a new garden with her. This process begins in Altai.

The journey to Mt Belukha will take the Fellowship deep into the center of their beings where the heart portal projects our spirit into physical form. From the depth of their beingness, their gratitude for the treasury of life experienced within them will awaken as an intention of love. This love will awaken the Altai portal. By holding open the heart and letting love radiate outward, the Altai portal will open and merge with the heart portal at the center of their being. The love from the mountain will enter their heart portal and radiate throughout their entire being. This process will be unique and specific to each person and the entire fellowship will support each person in their process.

Once the resonance has settled in, the group will come into sync. Then the group will come into sync with the intention of the mountain portal as it transmits the fifth dimensional ascension energies. Once this New Earth resonance settles in, then the intention will be to broadcast this frequency from a point above the mountain.This beacon will transmit from mountain top to mountain top around the globe where similar activations will take place at other portal sites. This mountain top grid will stay in place and continue transmitting into the New Age.

Even in places where portals are a distance away, the open hearted, loving intentions of the grounding group will receive the New Earth energies from the nearest mountain top. Their synchronicity with the mountain grid will be cleansing to themselves and their immediate surroundings of land and people. This synchronicity will also make the energy available to everyone who is sharing a heart connection to each participant.

This open resonance of receiving will enable the pathways of mineral and water to begin manifesting the New Earth intentions. These intentions will then be carried to the mountain lakes and broadcast to the heavens above. Clouds carrying the seeds of the love of life will rain upon the surface, beginning the germination of the New Earth frequencies. The New Earth frequency grid is available around the globe, whether a person is aware of it or not. Awareness will arise spontaneously as the frequency spreads. It will be a joy to witness and be part of!

2. Premonition by Maia Rose

A Communication with Altai's Beings of Light

May 14, 2011

This is an excerpt of a communication on behalf of the Altai Fellowship that came through with the help of Maia Rose, who is a member of the Altai Fellowship. A spokeswoman for the Fellowship of Light started communicating with Maia last fall. When asked, the Almas (Siberian Bigfoot people) also began communicating with her this spring. The rest of the communication will be shared with the Grounding Group before the July 30th Preparatory Call.

I am communicating with the Illuminated Beings.

I see members standing on white cliffs holding a white book. They, the mountain and the book all appear to be made of white light. A spokesperson steps forward to say: "We are glad to be here and glad to be asked to support your journey."

What is the nature of the energy portal to be opened in Altai this summer?

This portal is a place where there is a buildup of extra energy that vibrates at a higher frequency which makes it more concentrated, but less dense than the general energy field. I am seeing it as egg-shaped with the point at the top.

Where does this energy come from?

This Altai portal is a gift from the illuminated beings who brought it to these mountains many millennia ago so it could be preserved. There are also portals preserved in other places around the globe. This was done in cooperation with Gaia. The elevation and the minerals in the mountains preserve them. Gaia has been instrumental in deciding where the portals are. She is a spiritually evolved being who has chosen to incarnate as a planet. This is her body and she likes it when there is cooperation and harmony between the peoples and all beings who live on her.

In the same way that humans have tried to separate mind and body medically, people see themselves as separate from the planet. There is no separation between Gaia and the people and other beings who live on her. You are learning through medicine that the mind and body is an integrated process; they are not separate entities. It is also so, between you and Gaia. When things started to degrade and human society began to evolve separate from the Earth and the animal and plant spirits, the Illuminated Beings asked Gaia what to do with the light energy. She told them to store the energy in places with high mineral content, so it would be best preserved.

Where did the energy come from in the first place?

From Stars.

The portal is a cache of the energy of creation, originating from the God source.

How do we open this Cache?

Love.

I gave a very seemingly simple answer because the word love encompasses everything.

How should the energy be transmitted?

Do your best and use your intuition. Your intuition will be heightened when you get there and you will just know what to do. It doesn't have to be a dog and pony show; it doesn't' have to be song and dance. The most profound things are quiet and simple. That is why I said love, because love will take care of it all.

In a way it doesn't matter how the energy is transmitted. Some people may see an image, but it is not limited to a visual form. It might come through any sense. Somebody might hear it as the OM, somebody might feel a tickle on their side or they might feel peaceful or their heart may feel expanded. The limited consciousness of human's tries to make everything so small. Think of a fractal, based on a mathematical infinity— it just goes and goes and goes. God makes infinite numbers of flowers, all different kinds. The transmission of energy can be done in an infinite number of ways. Each person can choose one. If you are looking for one way to know God, you will be disappointed. God expresses herself/himself in infinite ways.

Also intention. (Meaning sensing the energy in some form and then setting an intention as to what to do with it.)

Now the wilderness beings (Almas / Bigfoot) in the mountains are saying: "If we know you intend to do this and you really want to do this, if you choose it, we will be glad to help. If you want it (and you do) and we want it (and we do), then it's a done deal." The most profound things can be simple, like a Rumi poem.

Is the Altai portal opening a part of a global transition?

Machu Picchu and other mountainous regions like the Himalayas also have energy caches, partly because the mountains are up high and partly because of the mineral content that stores the energy. (Metal is a conductor of energy including emotions and that's why, from time to time, metal jewelry needs to be energetically cleaned.) In rocky areas, the metal ores conduct energy.

To conduct the energy of light and love, the Illuminated Ones went to the mountains where the energy could be conducted and stored. Some of the other caches around the world are being opened. The openings will happen sequentially. The Illuminated Ones know when the time is right and will call people to come and open them because this needs to be a joint endeavor. Earth is a "free-will" planet so humans need to actively choose to do this.

Gaia has her own ideas about her life. She interacts with the beings on her as a very literal part of her. First there's soil. The seeds grow in the soil and then the animals eat the plants. The fish also eat the various substances of Gaia's body. So, our human bodies came from her. We are part of her. We are not separate from her. We are an integral part of her and she is an integral part of us. That is how synchronicity works, it is a mutual agreement between parts of the same whole.

What effect is the opening of the portal going to have on ourselves and our communities?

The effect on each person will be individual and it will be exactly what they want it to be because they will create it with their intention. It will look the way they want it and be how they want it.

The effect on the community will be the degree to which they act on their intuition. The more people act, the more the energy will flow through them.

How is this related to the ascension of the Earth?

The ascension of the Earth means that the vibrational frequency rises and along with it people's consciousness rise. When these portals open up around the globe, the energy brought in supports the ascension. The more light and unconditional love there is on Earth, the easier it will be.

Not only will Gaia and the atmosphere and the whole 3rd dimension be moving towards the 4th dimension, but people's consciousness will be expanding. The mind does not exist inside the brain, the brain exists inside the mind. The mind field will be vibrating faster and people will be sensing their interconnectedness more and have more kindness and unconditional love for each other. It is kindness, unconditional love, and wise mind knowing that will create the ascension; but these qualities will also be created by the ascension. Gaia is ascending whether we all go with her or not, that's where she's going, that is her intention.

Is there anything we can do to ease the suffering of Mother Earth and the life that she supports?

Well, stop thinking of her as suffering. Think of it as experiencing. Different individuals come into incarnation for different experiences. Everybody is having the experience that they more or less volunteered for. We don't have to see people as suffering or victims to be willing to help them. When you assist someone it benefits you also. People are experiencing that in Japan after the tsunami.

Like two cells in the body: they don't perceive each other as suffering or being a victim, they just work to come back into balance. You also don't have to be mean hearted and think "Well that person volunteered to have this experience, so I don't need to help." An aspect of opening the portal is to inspire action steps for sharing unconditional love. This will in turn increase the planetary vibration and thus the rate of ascension. If you think of it as suffering, the energy gets stuck in that concept and consequently has a lower vibrational level.

If you really think of Gaia as a woman in a planet body, she volunteered, too. Her lifetime is longer than a human lifetime, but she is a very spiritual woman having this planetary experience. So you can imagine that to her having an earthquake is like a human having the flu or getting physically out of balance in some other way. She suffers much more for lack of unconditional love than from any specific earth event. Remember that HAARP is doing some of the damage. And unconditional love is a way of addressing that too.

Is there anything else that we should let people know?

Everybody needs to play, play, play! Laugh, sing, dance, be goofy, hug. Some of the "right action" needs to be play! Do creative things, paint, draw, sing, if you are loving life you are living in "right action"!

It's all going to come right eventually. The balance will come eventually. Be optimistic. Like Uncle Harry Jim, the Kahuna says, "The gig is rigged." Gaia wants this, so we are going to get to balance somehow. Humanity's part of the ascension is to move into intuition and to reach out to amplify the connectedness that already exists.

The people in Japan are experiencing this beautifully because they don't have anything left, they are learning to use their intuition more and supporting each other.

Trust that everything is going to work out for the highest good. Use your intuition!

How will the energy of the portal opening be received, how should the Grounding Groups help?

(I See people sitting in their own spaces or in shared community spaces.) The more relaxed people are, the more energy they will be able to absorb. However, if you lay down, it will be harder to ground the energy into the Earth. Don't make the ceremony too long. Longer is not better. Afterwards, it would be good for people to walk quietly or be in quiet communion with themselves. Give grace to do what you are inspired to do. Walking around nature is good and then, after a while, come back together and share food.

Initially ground the energy into where you are sitting. The piece of earth you are sitting on. If you are sitting inside, send it down into the earth. If you are sitting in a flower-bed or garden, you can plant something there after. When it grows, it will include that energy. (Gold Star Meditation will connect with and ground the energy)

The receipt of the energy will increase intuition. Once the portal is open, it will remain open.

In the days and weeks following, you must continue to channel the energy in active ways. Each person will listen to their intuition to know what right action to do with the energy. Each person will have their own right action to do because we all have individual lives and birth plans. Whatever goodness, whatever mission that you came to do, use the energy to do it more and more.

The more you use the energy, the more it will transform your lives. More and more you will move beyond being solely emotional and solely reasonable into true Wisdom and Knowing. In time you will become this wisdom, 24/7. In future times, it will become impossible to reason things out fast enough to make a decision. Sequential reasoning will become too slow of a process. Decisions will instead need to be made through the wisdom of intuition.

Intuition is not the same as impulsiveness, intuition is based in the wisdom of global consciousness. Each person is a creative being and will have a different idea or inspiration: For example, my intuition is to plant bulbs, my intuition is to feed the homeless, my intuition is to work on getting the waterways cleared.

The people who download the energy will also connect in their own unique ways with the energy using different senses. Some may see a flash of light, hear a high-pitched humming or feel warmth or expansiveness.

Use mindfulness, notice and use your intuition, connect with everything around you, each leaf on a tree, a single ant, let everything be important and valuable. Be in gratitude for all things in your life. Just spread love, laugh and have a good time with others. This will raise people's energy.

High energy states or high vibrational states make manifestation easier. The easier it is for the majority of people to manifest the good; the more combined abundance there will be in the world.

What is optimal to do with the energy?

Take action with the energy to share it however it feels right to you. Flow. Be the river. The energy needs to be in motion. Do do do do! Don't think that any kindness is too small. If you can't do a big project, just do the little things you can do. Always be on the lookout for ways to connect and share love with others, birds, fish animals, fairies, almas, apes… Whatever you can do to honor the connection from a place of unconditional love.

The biggest source of "not doing" is shame. When people fear that they will feel shame or be embarrassed, they don't even try. In terms of practicing unconditional love, start with unconditional love of self in order to release and remove shame.

What effect is the opening of the portal going to have on ourselves and our communities?

The effect on each person will be individual and it will be exactly what they want it to be because they will create it with their intention. It will look the way they want it and be how they want it.

The effect on the community will be the degree to which they act on their intuition. The more people act, the more the energy will flow through them.

The Altai Fellowship is a self-selected international group that has come together for the purpose of opening an energy gate and transmitting this energy out into the world in the Altai Republic in Siberia July-August, 2011. This group is organized by Altai Mir University and led by Carol Hiltner, a Seattle-based author/artist/activist facilitating global flourishing of traditional wisdom.

The mission of Altai Mir University is to build peace by bridging ancient wisdom with today's world, primarily through leadership exchanges, events, and projects to strengthen indigenous cultures and their value to current global affairs. AMU is a US-based 501(c)3 nonprofit corporation.

On August 13, 2011, she and a group of fellow pilgrims including Maia Rose {and Krystal Kelley} will access the reserve cache of life force that has been stored in Altai by Mother Earth and the Brotherhood of Light, and transmit it globally to facilitate global spiritual opening. People around the world are needed to receive and ground this energy.

More information at www.altaifellowship.wordpress.com

3. Natural order

June 27, 2011 by Patricia Anne Davis, Choctaw-Navajo/ Chahta-Dineh Wisdom Keeper

The Natural Order

Affirmative Thinking System

The first thing to understand about the Navajo language is that it is spoken in an Affirmative thinking system within the natural order as described in the examples of time and cardinal direction correlated with blessing way principles moving clockwise.

Typically, English is spoken symbolically in a triangle and in a different thinking system. It is in the context of hierarchy, patriarchy and describes everyone in their deficient self-image, which must be remediated into some end-state of civilization or enlightenment.

English is abstract. It is a trade and commerce language. Navajo is descriptive and exact. Therefore, healing ceremonies are exact and actual in the natural order, which is not religion, philosophy or theory.

Open vs Closed Social System

Below, you will find a graphic representation of the transcendence that occurs when the Closed System of Disease

That is designed for failure is re-framed into the Open system of the Natural Order during the Ceremonial Change Process.

There are four phases to every healing process that leads to curing, not coping. Before defining them, one must know that the healing process does not exist in the English language thinking system, but it can be described to convey the integrity of the sacred meaning of Navajo words.

The term "Navajo" is an imposed name. We Dineh have several spiritual names that identify us to the creator as a precious child of divine creation, made of earth-physical, water-emotive, fire-mental and air-spiritual. Corn is the symbol of food as social medicine within the economic relationships of the clan system. Our spiritual names are inclusive and universal in application to all people. One name is "earth-surface people", another is "five-fingered" people and another is the affirmation: "I am a precious child of creator".

Consequences of Closed System Thinking

When a person makes decisions that are destructive and death-producing, this is considered misuse of thinking by using thinking for what it is not for. All ceremonies correct erroneous thinking that "tell" the body wrong information. Every out-of-balance condition is a consequence of saying "yes" to destructive and death-producing choices and saying "no" to constructive and life-affirming choices.

When a person denies the unifying principle that all creation is Inter-related, this is "stress". All of the diseases are a consequence of denying our oneness with the creator's will-to-love. All Navajo healing ceremonies restore a person to their true spiritual Self-identity as a precious child of creator made of the four sacred elements: air-spiritual; fire-mental; water-emotive; earth-physical body. When any one of these elements is out of balance, there is disease with creator's will-to-love that manifests as disease.

Living Hozho, in the Natural Order

The Navajo language is a spiritual language spoken with living words that manifest vibrations for affirming truth in the laws of nature or the natural order of time and direction from East-thinking, West-planning, South-decision making for collective survival and North-equity in restoring resources to the next generation moving clockwise within temporal time and cardinal direction.

For example: sunrise, mid-day, sunset, mid-night; spring, summer, fall, winter; child, youth, adult, and elder. Also, white people, red people, yellow people and black people, all born equal in the sacred circle of life within the holiness and wholeness of hozho. There is no concept of separation from creator or from the natural order. There is only the principle of making constructive and life-affirming choices.

Find more indigenous wisdoms from Patricia at nativeamericanconcepts.wordpress.com or on Facebook at Indigenous Wisdom Institute

4. Whole Brain Thinking

By Patricia Anne Davis, Choctaw-Navajo/Chahta-Dineh
Wisdom Keeper

Context: hozho natural order

Wisdom &knowledge-symbol-language-holy thinking-voice-words

The context for facilitating a ceremonial change process is hozho, an all encompassing concept of holiness and wholeness without competing collectivities and ideologies. The context of the natural order in hozho is represented by a symbol – a circle with an opening in the east direction with one inner circle moving counterclockwise representing the female nurturer gender life task; and an outer circle moving clockwise representing the protector-provider gender life task. These two circles can also be rearranged into a figure eight, the Infiniti symbol, which could further be combined into one circle, the eternity symbol. Everyone must have a language in order to think in that language. Whole-brain thinking is holy thinking and clear congruent thinking, synonymous with the sacred-SELF intellect. Thus, voice gives expression to the creator's holy breath through living words. This continuum is a holographic holistic thinking system.

The creator's holy breath is the miracle of photosynthesis. In the miracle of photosynthesis plants give us oxygen to breath and plants absorb the carbon-dioxide we exhale. Perfect love and peace from creator radiates to the physical sun. Sunrays radiate to the plants and we exchange oxygen and carbon dioxide with the plants in the miracle of photosynthesis. This is the creator's holy breath that gives life and voice to spoken living words. Voice expresses the sacred-SELF intellect through holy thinking.

Strategy

How this process works: creator informs the Real-SELF who informs the sacred-SELF for powerwithin to have powerwith others through an Indigenous ceremonial change process.

All my work is translated from the Navajo/Dineh language and those italicized words notate that. The meaning and vibration is my way of keeping track of information in English while I exist, speak and write in the Dineh Affirmative thinking system. For an explanation of the terms above, please visit the glossary

©Patricia Anne Davis, MA and the Navajo Nation Justice Department

Made in the USA
Monee, IL
22 May 2020

31393869R00069